2025–2026 EDITION

COLLEGE TRANSFER READY

EXPERT ADVICE FOR PARENTS TO SUPPORT THEIR STUDENT'S DECISION

EDITED BY

CHELSEA PETREE, Ph.D.

PARENT **READY.**

Table of Contents

This book is dedicated to the parents, siblings, family members, caregivers, mentors, and supporters of a unique and valuable population—transfer students.

Contributors

Editor

Chelsea Petree, Ph.D.
Rochester Institute of Technology

Chelsea Petree is the Parent and Family Programs director at Rochester Institute of Technology (RIT). Chelsea moved to Rochester in 2015 to establish the Parent and Family Programs office, including developing a comprehensive parent communications plan and implementing family events and engagement opportunities. She has worked to establish a "parents as partners" culture at RIT, increasing support of families across the institution. Chelsea received her Ph.D. in family social science from the University of Minnesota in 2013 and has served on the board of directors and as president of AHEPPP: Family Engagement in Higher Education. She has won several awards, including the 2019 Rising Alumni Award from the College of Education and Human Development at the University of Minnesota and the 2021 AHEPPP Powerful Partnership Award for Tiger Parent Project, a program that brings together RIT staff and faculty to learn more about the family experience and parent-student-university relationships. She is the editor of the College Ready book series.

Contributors

Eric Dusseault, Ph.D.
Emerson College

Eric Dusseault is senior director for the office of Student Success and Retention at Emerson College in Boston, Massachusetts. This office oversees many of the college's retention-based initiatives, including student leaves, returns, and transfer student support. Prior to his role at Emerson, Eric served as the assistant director of academic success programs in the Academic Resource Center at the Massachusetts College of Art & Design (MassArt). He also had professional appointments with the Rhode Island School of Design (RISD), the Massachusetts College of Liberal Arts (MCLA), and the Maryland Institute College of Art (MICA). Eric began his journey in educational support while holding various student leadership positions at Keene State College, where he earned a bachelor of arts in English with a minor in communication, which inspired him to pursue a master's in student affairs administration at Ball State University. While working at MassArt, Eric developed a peer advising model and oversaw student tutoring, teaching assistant and new faculty training, and major exploration programs. Eric earned his Ph.D. in higher education from the University of Massachusetts Boston in August 2024. Eric is also an illustrator and artist and holds two certificates, one in comic and sequential art and another in children's book illustration, from the Rhode Island School of Design, where he has taught the continuing education courses Foundation Drawing; Character Design: Might, Myth, and Magic; The Fairytale Workshop; and Biographical Illustration.

Rebecca D. Leonard, Ph.D.
Penn State University

Rebecca (Becki) Leonard brings almost 10 years of experience working with transfer students. Beginning her professional career as an academic adviser at Penn State Behrend in Erie, Pennsylvania, she supported students on both sides of the transition—those coming to the institution and those making plans to transfer out of the institution. In March 2022, she joined the Student Orientation and Transition Programs (SOTP) team at Penn State University Park in State College, Pennsylvania, as the assistant director for Transition Programs. In this role, she provided orientation, programming, and coaching for students transferring from external institutions to the campus, as well as students transitioning from a regional Penn State campus to the flagship campus. Becki now serves as the associate director in SOTP and provides leadership for orientation programming for first-year students at the University Park campus. She earned her Ph.D. from Notre Dame of Maryland University, where she focused her dissertation research on the experiences of students in transition. When she is not at work, Becki enjoys going on adventures with her partner, spending time with their two dogs, crafting, and reading.

Zoë Segnitz, M.A.
Boise State University

Zoë Segnitz has spent her career in a range of student support spaces and currently focuses on student transition, family engagement, and peer mentorship. Community building and learning in relationships define her endeavors. As the director of New Student Programs at Boise State University in Idaho, she leverages her highly collaborative work portfolio toward tightening cross-departmental partnerships, so that students experience their university home as one interconnected and supportive environment. In her time at Boise State, she has sought to refine and improve onboarding and mentorship for students based on population. Her strategic approach to onboarding and mentorship is informed by the dedicated study of specific student populations. A careful analysis of commuter student challenges led her to develop a peer mentorship program, pairing first-year students with experienced student leaders. This initiative has already boosted retention rates for participants by 14%. Beginning in fall 2025, this program will expand to include transfer students. Zoë's commitment to transfer student success is guided by the university's broader enrollment and retention strategies. She is currently adjusting services to capitalize on the convenience of virtual tools during the transition period, while improving the timing of community-building efforts to meet transfer students' unique needs. Equally passionate about family engagement, Zoë transformed Boise State's family orientation into one that highlights the value of learning in community. With the recent creation of a sustainable budget model for family programs, she has positioned the university to increase its engagement with families in the coming years. At every stage of her career, Zoë has been driven by a dedication to student-centered service, collaboration, and continuous improvement.

Shelitha W. Williams, Ed.D.
Rochester Institute of Technology

Shelitha Williams is a passionate advocate for student success with more than 25 years of experience in higher education. As the associate vice president of Student Affairs at Rochester Institute of Technology (RIT), she leads departments that collaborate with academic affairs to enhance student access and achievement. Shelitha spent 20 years in leadership roles within community colleges, where she championed initiatives to support students and create inclusive pathways to higher education. Throughout her career, she spearheaded the development of innovative departments and programs designed to bolster student support. An engaging speaker and consultant, Shelitha actively shares her insights and best practices with the higher education community. Her commitment to student success is deeply rooted in her own experience as a first-generation college student. She is a dedicated mentor and role model, inspiring students and colleagues alike to pursue their goals with resilience and determination. She is also passionate about guiding parents in navigating their student's academic journey, recognizing the vital role that families play in supporting student achievement. Shelitha earned a doctorate in educational leadership from the University of Rochester, a master's in social work from Stony Brook University, and a bachelor's in psychology from SUNY Potsdam. She finds daily inspiration in the students she serves, which fuels her dedication to creating environments where all students can thrive.

Introduction

This book is for the parents and families of transfer students, who began their journey at one institution and are embarking on a different path by enrolling at a new institution.

As the family member of a transfer student, you are familiar with the college process. You've been through the tour and application process; you attended orientation and perhaps moved your student in; and you cheered them on as they began this new chapter in their life. You've been here before! But as you have likely already learned, all colleges are different, and your student is going to have a new experience at this new institution—whether they are transferring after just a semester at their first school or have completed an associate degree at a community college and are moving on to a bachelor's program.

There are many reasons students transfer to a new college. They may have started at a community college with a well-considered plan to get some credits under their belt before moving to a four-year institution, or perhaps they wanted to explore a variety of general education courses for a semester or two to help them narrow in on a major. Or they may have started at their dream college only to realize the dream couldn't be fulfilled there because career goals or a financial situation changed or it didn't turn out to be the right place for them. The decision to transfer can be difficult after putting so much effort into choosing the first college. They might be nervous to tell you they aren't happy and want to make a change. But transferring colleges, whether to a community college back home or another four-year institution, is completely normal and can be the best way for your student to be successful.

Whatever the reason for transferring, it will take some effort on your student's part. Finding a new institution that is a better fit, completing the necessary paperwork and applications, and learning the systems of a new school can be daunting. Once they arrive at their new college, they will have to remember that, while they are an experienced student, they are new to this place, which can be confusing and create its own challenges. With support and encouragement from you, this process will feel a lot more manageable for your student.

This book is written by professionals who have worked closely with transfer students at their universities and throughout their careers. The content will help you support your student as they make this transition, find their place at their new university, and work their way toward graduation. The conversation starters at the end of the chapters can help you bring up challenging topics and have meaningful conversations around them.

Not all college students follow the same path, and there is not one right way to do college. Your student may already be well on the path to their new institution, or they may be just starting to consider the option to transfer. They may have experienced many of the issues in this book or none of them. Every student and family are different, and parts of the book will resonate differently with each reader. You will have your own experiences to contribute, and this book will provide perspective and guidance no matter your knowledge on each topic.

Finally, while this guide will support the transition itself, our other College Ready books (*College Ready, College Sophomore Ready, College Junior Ready,* and *Post-College Ready*) may also be valuable to help you understand what your student needs in terms of specific years. Wherever your student is on their transfer journey, College Ready is here for you!

Chelsea Petree, Ph.D.
College Ready **Editor**
Director, Parent & Family Programs
Rochester Institute of Technology

Chapter 1

WHY WOULD A
STUDENT TRANSFER?

Rebecca D. Leonard, Ph.D.
Penn State University

Your student has shared with you that they are considering transferring colleges. You may have seen this conversation coming, or it may feel like it came out of nowhere. It could happen during any year of your student's college journey. And it may spark questions within you: *Why did they choose this college in the first place? Are they making a mistake wanting to transfer? Do they have a reasonable motive for transferring?* While your student may have selected their current college after months of research and earnest decision-making, sometimes the institution they chose is not a good fit. Transferring colleges may be the difficult but necessary step your student needs to take toward finding an environment that supports their aspirations. This chapter will share some common reasons students choose to transfer—some of which may resonate with you and your student's situation—and provide suggestions for conversations to have with your student before they begin researching the next step in their college career.

When the College Isn't a Good Fit

Your student may come to you with specific reasons they need to transfer. However, sometimes they may not be able to pinpoint exactly what is wrong with their experience and say, "It just isn't a good fit." It can be difficult to offer help when your student is not able to explain exactly why their college is not a good fit. They may just have a gut feeling they can't quite articulate. Your student's desire to transfer is valid, even if it is based simply on a feeling. Through conversation and reflection, you can help your student work to understand what about the fit isn't quite right. While there are many factors that could be at play with fit, they can be put into three categories, discussed in the following paragraphs:

1. The physical campus
2. A sense of belonging
3. The academic experience

These categories can help guide your conversations with your student to help them evaluate what is and isn't good about the fit of their current college.

The Physical Fit

Your student's experience with the physical campus can significantly influence their comfort and overall feeling toward the institution. Your student likely visited campus before committing to attend the college, but experiencing a place all day, every day gives a different perspective than a daylong visit. Now that your student has a better understanding of the physical campus, they are well-equipped to analyze what they do and do not like about it.

Consider where the college is located in relation to home. Your student may have chosen the institution because it was far away from home or because it was close. For some students, the novelty of being far away quickly wears off once the semester starts, and they are left with the realization that being closer to family would be better for them. For other students, staying close to home may not give them the independence they crave, and they may want to try being on their own.

If your student's college is in a different climate than what they are used to, they may be dissatisfied with their day-to-day experience. This may be especially true for students who are used to year-round warm climates who attend college in a geographic location that can be blustery in the winter. Climate can affect your student's mood, mental health, and ability to thrive.

Whether the institution is in an urban or rural setting can influence how your student feels. They may find a bustling urban environment distracting and need a quieter, more rural setting. Or they may feel isolated and bored in a rural setting and feel they need a college in a more urban environment.

The size of the college may also influence their sense of fit. If your student is seeking personalized attention, a large campus with a sizable student population may feel overwhelming. (The feeling of being a little fish in a big pond is very real!) On the other hand, your student may feel that a small student body is too limiting, and they would prefer an environment that has more variety and opportunities to meet many people.

The Social Fit

Social life is an important part of the college experience and can have a significant impact on whether your student feels like they are a true member of their campus community. Your student may feel dissatisfied with their social life at their current college because they have a hard time making friends or have not found activities they enjoy. Your student may feel shy or intimidated by established friend groups or feel overwhelmed by the various events on campus. When students are not connected to their peers and organizations on campus, they can feel isolated. Many students find connection and fulfillment outside the classroom by participating in athletics, student government, clubs, performing arts, and other activities. If your student's current college does not offer activities that they are passionate about, your student may feel disconnected from campus life and want to transfer to an institution that can provide the cocurricular experience they desire.

Your student's sense of belonging on campus could be tied to whether they feel their identities are supported and celebrated. This may be especially true for students who belong to historically marginalized populations; if they do not feel their college values their identities, they may feel out of place on campus. The support and programs offered to students from different backgrounds, cultures, and identities vary widely from college to college, and your student's current college might not be meeting their needs. Similarly, your student may feel that their identity or identities are not represented within the larger student body. Hispanic-serving institutions (HSIs), historically Black colleges and universities (HBCUs), Tribal colleges and universities (TCUs), Alaska Native-serving institutions (ANSIs), and Native Hawaiian-serving institutions (NHSIs) are designations from the U.S. Department of Education. Your student may feel that transferring to an institution with one of these classifications will allow them to experience a greater sense of belonging and support.

Understanding the values that are prevalent on campus comes with time and experience, and your student may feel there is a misalignment between their personal values and the values of the campus community. This can mean differences in political views, social justice issues, or religious affiliation. It can also mean a misalignment in terms of expectations for things like partying and alcohol use. If your student feels that the values of the campus culture are at odds with their own, they may feel uncomfortable and seek to transfer to an institution that better aligns with their values.

The Academic Fit

It is important that your student feels the academic environment of their college aligns with their goals. There are a few reasons the academic environment may fall short of your student's expectations.

Class sizes can affect how well your student is able to engage with the material, their peers, and their instructors. A student who thrives in a small, discussion-based learning environment may struggle to find success in a large lecture hall. Alternatively, students who prefer larger classes may feel constrained by the intimacy of smaller ones. Now that your student has some time under their belt at their current college, they can reflect on whether the class sizes allow them to do their best.

Your student may feel the coursework is either too challenging or not challenging enough, both of which can lead to dissatisfaction inside the classroom. If your student is struggling in classes but support does not appear to be available, they may feel frustrated and wish to transfer to an institution that has the services they need. The level of resources provided—like tutoring, writing centers, or disability services—as well as their comfort in using these services can affect your student's academic experience.

If your student has discovered a particular interest in conducting research and that is not an option provided to them at their current college, they may want to transfer to a more research-oriented institution. Colleges that have robust research programs can engage students and provide hands-on experiences in their field, which can be especially useful if your student is considering pursuing graduate school.

When Major or Career Goals Change

One of the most common reasons for transferring is a change in major or career goals. Your student may have chosen their current college because it has a great reputation in their intended field of study or offers great outcomes for its graduates. However, when their intended major changes, these elements can change, too. For example, your student may be considering a new major that their current college does not offer. They can stay at their current college and work with an academic advisor to discuss how to tailor their coursework, but they may feel more comfortable pursuing their true desired major at a new institution. Or your student might be changing into a major that is offered at their current institution, but they know that another college has a bigger or more prestigious department for their new major. Transferring to such a college may open doors to internships, research opportunities, and future employment. Staying in a program that does not align with their new goals may be frustrating, so transferring may be the best option.

Career services are a vital part of preparing for life after college. If your student's current school does not provide support for their new field of interest after graduation, they may consider transferring. Some institutions provide specialized internship programs or job placement services, which could be a perk of changing institutions. Similarly, the location of your student's college could influence their ability to land their dream job or internship. Some fields, such as finance, entertainment, or technology, can be concentrated in specific geographic areas, so attending a college in close proximity to those areas could be advantageous.

When Family or Personal Reasons Come into Play

Sometimes, the decision to transfer institutions has less to do with the college and more to do with personal or family circumstances. A family member's health crisis, a divorce, or other changes in family dynamics can make focusing on school difficult, especially if the institution is far away from home. Your student may also find that their current college situation makes it difficult to maintain relationships with a significant other or close friends, which can influence their sense of belonging both at school and at home. Transferring institutions may allow your student to balance their college experience with being present for the important people in their life in a way that is most comfortable for them.

Mental health and homesickness can also influence a student's desire to transfer. College can be overwhelming. Dealing with issues such as anxiety, depression, stress, and homesickness may get in the way of academic and social experiences. If their college does not provide the mental health support they need, transferring to an institution with better services and wellness programs may improve your student's well-being. See page 21 in Chapter 2 for more on creating a checklist to conduct research for a new institution.

When Money Talks

The cost of college is significant, and there could be a number of financial reasons your student chooses to transfer.

- If your student's college increases tuition, they may want a school that more closely aligns with their budget.

- If your student loses a scholarship or grant, continuing at the current college may not be financially possible; they may find a better financial aid package elsewhere.

- If family finances change unexpectedly, due to job loss or medical expenses, your student may need a more affordable school.

- If your student needs to work an on- or off-campus job but can't find the right opportunities, they might want to transfer to a college with more employment options.

Closing Advice

The decision to transfer colleges is a deeply personal one. Your student's situation may or may not fit into one of the areas discussed in this chapter. As a parent, approaching the "transfer" conversation with empathy and understanding will help your student through this journey. By considering factors such as campus fit, academics, family and personal reasons, and finances, you can support your student in making a well-informed decision that will help them thrive.

Conversation Starters

- How can we, as your family, support you through this decision-making process?

- What were your initial expectations when you chose your current college? Have those expectations changed and, if so, how?

- What specific experiences or events have led you to feel like transferring might be the right choice?

- How would transferring affect:

  - Your long-term career goals?

  - Your academic experience?

  - Your financial situation?

  - Your personal and mental well-being?

  - Your involvement and sense of belonging on campus?

Chapter 2

HOW DOES A STUDENT TRANSFER?

Eric Dusseault, Ph.D.
Emerson College

Transferring from one college to another is a significant decision that requires careful thought and planning. Whether a student is feeling unfulfilled academically, struggling socially, or dealing with financial concerns, the reasons for wanting to transfer are varied and personal. Before making the leap, it's crucial to assess the situation thoroughly and explore options that can improve the student's current experience. By reflecting on their challenges and needs, students can better determine whether transferring is the right path and how to navigate the process effectively. This chapter will help you and your student consider the most important factors before deciding to transfer, ensuring they are well-prepared and informed every step of the way. We start by asking one simple question.

"Are You Happy?"

This question can be difficult for anyone to answer, but it can be especially challenging for a college student who is considering transferring to another institution. While the reasons for transferring vary—financial burdens; social challenges like roommate conflicts, relationship breakups, or feelings of isolation; and disappointments like not making the varsity team or achieving good grades—the root of the issue often comes down to one simple statement from the student: I'm not happy here.

As a parent, hearing this can be heartbreaking, frustrating, or both. After all, you likely spent a lot of time touring colleges, completing applications, talking with administrators, and connecting with other parents. You might even have read books like the one you're reading now. How could this happen when you did everything right, despite all the careful planning and effort you made to set up your student for success? In this moment, it can be tempting to console, coddle, or even admonish them.

You are likely thinking, "What do you mean you're not happy? Who's responsible for this? Who do I need to call to get you more support? You wanted to be here!" While your initial impulse will be to react immediately, it is better to take a moment to pause and shift your mindset before engaging in this conversation. It will be more helpful for both you and your student to stay curious and ask your student to share more about their challenges. Sometimes, the simple phrase "say more" can open the door to a deeper conversation.

If your student isn't making the social connections they expected, they may feel isolated or out of place. They may express financial concerns, feeling guilty or anxious about the burden of tuition on you or accumulating debt. Another common reason to want to transfer is mental health. College can be overwhelming, especially for students who have grown up in a time of school shootings and active shooter drills. Social media adds to this pressure, creating a sense of being under constant scrutiny and not living up to expectations. When your student opens up about their reasons for wanting to transfer, it gives you the opportunity to help them reflect on what's really at the root of their unhappiness. From there, you can guide them in navigating their next steps. Remember that your role isn't necessarily to fix the problem but to help your student think beyond the immediate situation and toward their future. By talking through their concerns together, they may find solutions they hadn't considered, which could allow them to stay and grow in ways they hadn't expected.

However, in some cases, transferring may indeed be the best option.

The Decision Is Made

As mentioned in Chapter 1, transferring is not an admission of failure or an inability to adapt to college life; it's often a sign of maturity— a recognition that your student's needs aren't being met and that another institution might offer a better environment for them to thrive. For example, imagine your student entered a large university on a premed track, feeling certain about becoming a doctor. However, during their first year, they discovered a passion for filmmaking, especially documentary creation, while taking an elective course. As they dove deeper into the craft, they realized that storytelling through film resonated more with their interests and skills than their original path. Unfortunately, their current college doesn't offer a dedicated film studies or documentary program. Transferring would give your student the opportunity to fully explore this path, potentially setting them up for a more fulfilling career in a field they are genuinely excited about.

While the decision to transfer can be difficult, it's important to support your student in finding an environment that best aligns with their evolving goals and aspirations. After all, a major reason to attend college is for your student to find their path and passion, and it's exciting when it happens. It is not uncommon for students to enter a college or university with a predetermined major and to graduate with a different one. It is often not until they are exposed to the reality of the major and what it entails that they become more informed about what they wish to study and pursue.

Many students begin considering a transfer long before they mention it to their parents. For some, transferring might even have been part of the plan all along—whether it was a strategy to get into a dream school or a decision to attend their current institution for a few years and move on. The motivations vary, but, most often, it comes down to a sense of belonging and happiness.

Start the Conversation

There are a number of offices that your student will have to connect with after the decision is made to transfer. There are also several offices that can help your student make the decision. You can not only help your student generate a list of people to talk with, but you can also help them brainstorm questions to ask.

Academic Advisors

Transfer conversations should start with an academic advisor. Academic advising is a key resource at most colleges and universities. Advisors are trained professionals who can help students plan their academic journey, including discussing transfer options. By the time a student meets with an advisor, they've likely already talked with you about their desire to transfer. The advisor's role is not to dissuade the student from leaving, but to listen to the student's concerns, offering resources that might help them see their options more clearly. Academic advisors can identify and offer solutions to perceived issues that can help the student explore different options. During this meeting, or perhaps afterward, a student may decide it is in their best interest to remain at their current institution, knowing they have options and are more in control of their educational experience than they may have realized. On the other hand, the student may feel more certain that transferring is the right move. Either outcome is okay.

The academic advisor can work with the student on developing a timeline for transfer and navigating timing. Depending on when in the semester the student decides to transfer, it might be worthwhile to complete the current set of registered courses with the anticipation of transferring credits. Withdrawing from two or more courses in a semester may trigger certain bureaucratic events at the student's institution, such as the ability to remain in student housing or keep financial aid and scholarships. The student should be made aware of these potential pitfalls by the academic advisor before withdrawing from courses. Additionally, the academic advisor can ensure that the student has completed all the necessary paperwork and has a plan in place, particularly if the student should ever want or need to return. The student may feel more confident in their decision to explore another pathway if they are aware of the steps needed to return—just in case.

Friends and Mentors

While there are many individuals a student can consult, it's important to broaden the conversation beyond just academic advising when considering a transfer. Trusted friends, coaches, or supervisors can offer valuable perspectives if they know your student well and have insight into their strengths, challenges, and aspirations. These individuals can provide emotional support and help your student think critically about whether the transfer aligns with their long-term goals, both academically and personally. In some cases, spiritual leaders or mentors might be helpful in guiding students through the deeper, values-based considerations of making a major life change, offering a grounding presence as they weigh their options.

Financial Offices

Beyond personal and emotional support, it's essential for students to have follow-up conversations with financial aid officers and admissions counselors at both their current and prospective institutions. Speaking with a financial aid officer is crucial for understanding how transferring may impact your student's financial situation. This includes discussing whether current scholarships, grants, or loans will carry over to the new institution and whether there are any new funding opportunities available. Financial aid considerations can significantly influence the decision to transfer, as students need to ensure they can afford their new path without jeopardizing their financial well-being.

Admissions Counselors

Admissions counselors at the prospective institution are equally important in this process. They can help your student understand transfer requirements, including deadlines, application materials, and how their current credits will transfer. It is important that your student look specifically at the institution's transfer admissions page, as the process is different than for first-year admissions. Deadlines to apply will vary by institution and intended start semester but tend to be around March for a fall start and November for a spring start. While the application may look the same as that for applying first-year students, transfer students will likely also need to include a transcript from the institution from where are transferring. This is why it is necessary to pay close attention to transfer-specific admissions requirements and work with an admissions counselor so nothing is missed. This helps avoid any surprises regarding course equivalencies or lost credits, which could delay graduation. Moreover, admissions counselors can offer a realistic picture of what it will take for your student to succeed at the new institution, ensuring that the college truly fits your student's academic and extracurricular needs.

By involving these additional people and having practical conversations about finances and admissions, your student can make a decision that considers all aspects of their transition. This holistic approach ensures that they are not only following their passion, but they are also set up for success in all other areas of their college experience.

Generate a Checklist of Needs

Once your student has met with an academic advisor and reflected on their experience, the next step is to create a checklist of criteria for their next institution. This list, like the one they made when they were narrowing down college choices while in high school, should include the specific needs they've identified, as well as preferences that could be negotiable. For instance, some students know they need a smaller institution to be successful, while for others, size doesn't matter as much as location or availability of a specific major. This is all personal, and your student's experience at their first institution puts them in a better place to truly know what the negotiable and nonnegotiable factors are. Your student can learn about resources available at a new institution by touring campus, researching websites, and contacting staff. By creating a list, your student can clearly define what they're looking for and use it as a guide when researching potential transfer schools. It will also help them ask more informed questions when speaking with transfer admissions counselors. See Chapter 3 for a detailed checklist.

Initiate Contact with Potential Institutions

Armed with their checklist, your student can start researching potential schools. Online resources like the U.S. Department of Education's College Navigator or websites like Niche.com are great places to start. Following the social media accounts of prospective schools can give your student insight into the campus culture, and attending transfer-specific events can provide a chance to connect with current students. As a parent, it may be reassuring to know that the transfer process is often less stressful than the initial college application process. Much of the preparation is similar, though your student will need to pay attention to specific transfer requirements and deadlines.

Managing Expectations

Once your student has successfully transferred, it's important to manage expectations. Some students believe that transferring will solve all their problems, but some challenges may persist. Encourage your student to reflect on any recurring issues and how they might address them in their new environment.

If the new institution offers a transfer orientation, it's in their best interest to attend. This will help them meet peers and learn more about their new school. Transfer students should also be aware that they may be the last to register for courses or secure housing, so patience and flexibility are key during this transition. Ultimately, transferring can be a positive step, but it's important for students to approach it with realistic expectations and a proactive mindset.

Closing Advice

Transferring colleges is not an easy decision, but it can be the right one when done thoughtfully and with purpose. By carefully evaluating academic programs, financial implications, social dynamics, and long-term goals, students can make a decision that best supports their personal and educational growth. It's essential to approach the process with patience, keeping in mind that transferring is not a failure, but rather an opportunity for a fresh start. Remind your student that the key to a successful transfer lies in understanding and advocating for their needs, ensuring that the next institution offers the right environment for them to thrive. By creating and following a checklist and considering all aspects of the process, students can confidently move forward in their educational journey.

Conversation Starters

- What makes you happy at your current school?
- What is making you unhappy?
- Have you talked to your academic advisor about transferring? Who else have you spoken with?
- What schools are you looking at? How did you choose those schools?
- What are some first steps you can take to start this process?

Chapter 3

QUESTIONS TO CONSIDER WHEN TRANSFERRING

Eric Dusseault, Ph.D.
Emerson College

As you read in the first two chapters, there is a lot to think about when making the decision to transfer to a new college. As you guide your student through the process, this chapter can serve as a resource to ensure they consider all aspects of the transfer and ask the appropriate questions.

Academic Fit

- **Programs and Majors:** Does the new institution offer the academic program or major my student is seeking?

- **Course Credits:** Will current credits transfer? If so, how many and how will they apply to the new program? Is there a minimum grade that must be earned for credits to successfully transfer?

- **Graduation Timeline:** Does transferring delay my student's graduation date? If so, what is the impact and potential new timeline?

- **Class Availability:** Will my student have access to required courses after transfer? Are these classes often full or difficult to register for?

Financial Considerations

- **Tuition and Fees:** What is the cost of attendance (including tuition, fees, and room and board)?

- **Scholarships and Financial Aid:** Does my student qualify for financial aid or scholarships at the new institution? Does my student's current financial aid transfer?

- **Hidden Costs:** Are there additional costs (application fees, housing deposits, transfer fees) associated with transferring?

- **Student Loans:** How will transferring affect my student's loan situation? Will my student need to borrow more?

Social and Cultural Fit

- **Campus Size:** Will my student feel comfortable with the size of the new campus (large university vs. small college)?

- **Location:** Is the new institution in a location that suits my student (urban, suburban, rural)?

- **Social Scene:** Does the school offer clubs, activities, or organizations that match my student's interests?

- **Support Networks:** Do students have access to mental health services, career services, and student groups?

- **Housing:** Are there housing options available for transfer students? Is on-campus housing guaranteed?

Transfer Admissions Process

- **Transfer Application Deadlines:** What are the deadlines for applying to transfer? Where can they be found?

- **Required Documents:** What documents does a transfer student need to provide (transcripts, letters of recommendation, personal statement)? Does the institution require an official transcript? If so, what is the deadline for submitting one?

- **Transfer Orientation:** Does the new school offer an orientation or program for transfer students?

Academic Support and Resources

- **Advising:** Is there dedicated advising for transfer students? Can my student meet with an advisor before transferring?

- **Tutoring and Academic Support:** Are there resources available if my student needs help with a class (writing centers, tutoring, etc.)?

- **Career Services:** Does the new institution have strong career services and connections to internships or job opportunities in my student's proposed field?

Extracurricular and Social Opportunities

- **Clubs and Activities:** Are there extracurricular opportunities that align with my student's hobbies or interests?

- **Athletics:** If my student is involved in sports, will they be able to continue participating at the new school? If tryouts are required, how can my student initiate this process?

Long-Term Goals

- **Future Plans:** How will transferring impact my student's long-term goals (career plans, graduate school, etc.)?

- **Alumni Network:** Does the school have a strong alumni network that could help with future career opportunities?

Exit Strategy from Current Institution

- **Withdrawal Process:** What is the official withdrawal process at my student's current institution?

- **Impact on Current Standing:** Will withdrawing mid-semester affect my student's GPA or academic standing?

Reentry Plan

- **Return Option:** If the transfer doesn't work out, can my student return to their current institution? What steps would be needed for that?

Chapter 4

IS COMMUNITY COLLEGE A BETTER FIT?

Shelitha W. Williams, Ed.D.
Rochester Institute of Technology

Is your student considering transferring to a community college? It's a choice more families are exploring, and for good reason. Community colleges offer a supportive learning environment, affordable tuition, and flexible pathways, whether the goal is eventually a four-year degree or a direct career start. Community colleges cater to diverse learning journeys and career aspirations. This chapter will help you understand the benefits and factors to consider in transferring to a community college, so you can guide your student toward a thoughtful, informed decision.

What Is Community College?

Community colleges, also called junior or technical colleges, are two-year institutions with diverse programs designed to meet different educational goals. For students planning to continue their education at a four-year university, community colleges offer transfer-focused degrees such as the associate of arts (AA) and associate of science (AS). These programs cover general education requirements and basic courses, allowing students to transfer to a bachelor's program with some credits already completed. For students interested in entering the workforce quickly, career-focused associate degrees, certificates, and diplomas provide specific skills for fields like health care, technology, skilled trades, and business. The associate of applied science (AAS) and associate of occupational science (AOS) degrees, for example, can lead to careers in in-demand industries like cybersecurity, automotive technology, and health care.

Community colleges offer other programs and services:

- Microcredentials: Short, focused programs that develop high-demand skills in areas like digital marketing or project management

- Developmental education: Courses for students who need extra academic support to succeed in college-level classes

- GED preparation: Programs to help individuals earn a high school equivalency diploma

- Continuing education: Noncredit workshops and courses for personal or professional growth, covering topics from software skills to cooking and creative writing

With such a variety of programs, community colleges provide accessible, flexible options for students with different goals, whether they aim to transfer to a university, enter a career, or explore new fields.

Here's an overview of what students can expect from a community college experience:

Smaller Classes

Compared to courses held in lecture halls, community colleges often have smaller class sizes, promoting a collaborative learning environment where students can engage with instructors and classmates.

Support Services

Community colleges offer comprehensive resources like academic advising, tutoring, and career counseling. These services help students succeed in their studies, manage their career goals, and navigate challenges.

Flexible Schedules

With evening, weekend, and online courses, community colleges cater to students juggling education with work or family commitments. This flexibility lets students tailor their schedules to meet their personal needs.

Affordability

Community college tuition is substantially lower than that of four-year universities, which can reduce financial stress. In some states, community colleges are tuition-free for eligible students, making higher education more accessible than ever. A simple search on Google or community college websites will help you and your student understand if they qualify for free tuition in each state.

Community College Pathways

There are two common pathways that students will take in attending community college. Students who begin at a community college for two years and then transfer to a university for the final two years of a bachelor's program follow what's known as the 2+2 model. This path reduces overall tuition and lets students start their academic journey in a supportive, less costly environment. It's important to work with advisors to understand transfer agreements and ensure that credits will apply seamlessly at the university level. Even though these students will enter their bachelor's programs with college experience, the advice provided in this book will help them make the most of their final years at a new university.

Some students start at a four-year university and then transfer to a community college. This reverse transfer option can help those looking to save on tuition, find additional academic support, or explore different fields before deciding on a major. For students who need a more flexible or supportive setting, transferring "back" to community college can be an empowering, strategic choice.

Benefits and Limitations of Community College

Community colleges offer distinct advantages that make them a compelling choice, but there are also limitations to consider.

Benefits

- Cost savings: With state programs and financial aid, some students attend tuition-free.

- Major exploration: Students can explore subjects and career fields without committing to a major immediately. Advisors and faculty members are there to support students in discovering interests and strengths.

- Skill building: Students gain essential skills, such as critical thinking, communication, and teamwork, which are valued by employers.

- Real-world experience: Partnerships with local businesses and organizations mean internships and hands-on opportunities, providing students with practical experience and industry connections.

- Second chances: For students who may not have excelled in high school or who faced academic challenges at a university, community colleges offer an opportunity to build a strong academic foundation and prove their capabilities.

Limitations

- Specialized programs: Students with highly specific career paths may need to plan for earlier transfer options, because community colleges may lack certain specialized programs or majors offered at larger universities.

- Cocurricular variety: Students seeking an extensive campus life with clubs and residence-based activities may find fewer options at a community college.

- Transfer variability: Students need to work closely with academic advisors and be proactive in understanding credit transfer policies, because not all courses will transfer seamlessly to every four-year institution.

Is Community College the Right Fit?

Consider these potential advantages and limitations as your student determines if community college is the right fit for their needs. Below is a list of essential factors to consider.

Academic Goals

Community colleges cater to students pursuing both associate and bachelor's degrees. For those who may be undecided, community college offers an affordable setting to explore interests. For specialized fields, however—such as specific engineering disciplines—it's crucial to confirm that the community college offers relevant courses and that credits will transfer. Many community colleges have established transfer agreements with four-year universities, which can make the transition to a bachelor's degree program more seamless. These agreements often guarantee admission to specific schools or programs, provided you meet certain academic requirements.

Financial Considerations

Community colleges are generally more affordable than four-year universities. Many states also provide reduced or free tuition for eligible community college students, significantly decreasing the financial burden on families and reducing or eliminating student loan debt.

Learning Preference

With smaller class sizes and often greater access to instructors, community colleges may offer a more personalized educational experience. This can benefit students who thrive with more direct support or find large lecture hall environments challenging.

Campus Environment

Community colleges typically foster a close-knit, commuter-friendly environment. However, a growing number of community colleges offer residence halls, allowing students to experience a traditional college setting with the option of living on campus. For students looking for independence, an immersive campus life, or a taste of university living, this residential option can provide a valuable experience without the higher costs of a four-year institution.

University Readiness

Community colleges can be an excellent pathway for students who want to build academic skills, gain confidence, or take time to clarify their goals before committing to a four-year university. For students who are still finding their footing, community colleges provide an ideal space to mature academically and personally.

Addressing Common Concerns

Community colleges offer high-quality education, but there are still some misconceptions; common concerns are listed below.

Academic Rigor

Community colleges maintain rigorous academic standards, and many faculty members also teach at four-year universities and have valuable industry experience. Instructors are often focused on teaching and share their hands-on experience directly with students in their classes.

Social Life

While community colleges may not have the extensive cocurricular options of large universities, they do offer clubs, organizations, and events that provide valuable social engagement. Community colleges foster social connections through these clubs and events and have a vibrant campus life.

Stigma

Perceptions about community college are changing, and there is less negative stigma attached to this type of education than there was in the past. Today, they are increasingly recognized as a legitimate way to start a bachelor's degree or fulfilling career. Many successful professionals, including business leaders, health care providers, and technology experts, started their education at community colleges.

Making the Most of the Community College Experience

You can help your student make the most of their community college experience. Encourage them to establish good study habits and take advantage of resources like tutoring centers and writing labs, because academic success in community college is a strong foundation for university transfer or career goals. Encourage your student to join clubs, attend events, and connect with classmates. These experiences build confidence, community, and even lifelong friendships.

If a four-year degree is the ultimate goal, your student should work with advisors early to ensure courses align with transfer requirements. Research potential universities and understand their transfer credit policies to maximize efficiency and prevent issues.

Closing Advice

Community college offers a high-quality education, cost savings, and a supportive pathway to future success. It's a flexible option that empowers students to explore their academic interests, build confidence, and create a solid foundation for whatever path they choose. By considering the factors outlined in this chapter, you can guide your student toward an informed decision about their educational journey. Whether your student's goals include saving money, exploring majors, gaining valuable skills, or building a foundation for a university transfer, community college can be a smart starting point that opens doors to exciting future possibilities.

Conversation Starters

- What are your thoughts about transferring to community college?

- How might you learn better in smaller classes, like those often found at community colleges?

- What do you think about taking some semesters at community college to strengthen your grades?

- How important to you is saving money on tuition and reducing potential debt?

- How might starting at a community college build your skills and confidence before going to a university?

Chapter 5

HOW CAN A TRANSFER STUDENT FIND SUCCESS?

Zoë Segnitz, M.A.
Boise State University

Years from now, when your student is a college graduate and this tough transition is a thing of the past, do you know what they will say they learned from their first college experience? Reframing "what went wrong" as "what was learned" can help you and your student focus on finding a productive path forward. Even if this transfer was planned from the beginning of their college experience, your student has likely learned a thing or two that will help them be more successful in the future, and it can be beneficial to consider those lessons. Earning a college degree invites graduates to truly become learners who can log all life experiences, good and bad, as data gathered and insight gained. If you and your student can identify some lessons gained from this ongoing journey, it will be easier to let go of any lingering feeling of failure and lean into the pride of persevering. This chapter will provide insight into how to assist your student in thinking ahead and making their second college experience a successful one.

Focus on Lessons Learned

Watching your student suffer setbacks can make it tempting to focus on what might go wrong next. When you see your student go through a difficult time, it's normal to seek ways to protect them from future pain. Your first reaction might be to try to fix something or tell them what they need to do next. But rather than jumping in, help your student learn from the first college experience, considering what didn't work or go as well as it could have and what they need to change in this next experience to find the support and community they didn't have in the last. Your student is likely to feel more confidence and agency as they enter this next chapter if they can take ownership of their experience and pursue what they now know they need to be successful.

As you've read in the previous chapters, the "why" behind your student's transfer makes a difference in how they move forward and can reframe the experience now. Below are two examples of how a student might move forward once transferring, based on their reason for moving to a new institution.

Transferring for Social Reasons

Lexi entered her first semester ready to break free from the shadow of her charismatic first-born sister. But she hadn't developed the skills to make the social life she dreamed of a reality for herself. Despite being clear on what she wanted, she played it safe; in her own words, she really needed to "get over herself" and "embrace the awkward" so she could meet people. But she didn't. Instead, her feelings of isolation and despair intensified until she couldn't do it anymore, and she transferred at the end of her first term.

When she started again as a transfer student, she understood that her first institution had not been the problem. This time, she dug deep and threw herself into student leadership opportunities, embraced her vulnerability, and watched it pay dividends. Lexi was able to recognize what didn't work for her at her first institution and the role she played in it—not putting herself out there to find community. Rather than beating herself up or blaming her first institution, she made the most of starting over at a new school by joining clubs, trying new things, and ensuring she would have a better social experience.

Transferring for Academic Reasons

Kristin arrived at her second college home having left the first after realizing that it didn't offer the degree path she wanted. She arrived frustrated with herself and embarrassed that she wasted time and money. One year later, Kristin had a different story to tell. She had quickly realized that what she really learned through her not-perfectly-smooth start to college was how to be her own best advocate. Kristin began to see that her role wasn't just to attend classes, but also to actively shape her educational experience. She learned to reflect on her strengths, interests, and motivations and sought out the support and resources she needed. Empowered, she built meaningful relationships with professors, her advisor, and her on-campus supervisor, who helped guide her through this new phase of her college journey. By the time she graduated, Kristin's commitment to her own growth had yielded powerful results. She had developed a network of mentors who encouraged her, alerted her to new opportunities, and happily recommended her for prestigious scholarships and graduate programs. Her journey from frustration to fulfillment transformed her college experience into the foundation for lifelong success.

Perhaps transferring for academic reasons feels easier ("They didn't have the major I wanted!"), but students like Kristin still have opportunities to learn from their experiences and move forward. Kristin did not let the challenges of the transfer drag her down, and she instead made the most of her time in college by advocating for herself and building relationships across campus.

Recognize This as a New Experience

Some transfer students show up to new student orientation looking "over it" before they even begin. Some unapologetically ask how soon they can leave. Road weary and maybe even a little bruised up, their second college most likely doesn't look nearly as bright and shiny as the first one did—the one that ended up not working out. Or, for those who planned to transfer, they arrive with a "been there, done that" mentality.

While it's hard to act as if your second rodeo is your first, it's important to recognize that this is a new experience. Each university has its own environment, community, and personality, and while you and your student learned a lot in the first go-round, that's no reason not to be present for new opportunities. Transfer students can take their lessons learned and apply them at their new institution:

- What was missing from that experience that they can find here?

- What were the questions they didn't ask or resources they didn't find?

- What was lacking in the first community that drew them to this one?

Take Good Risks

Some transfer students seem to take pride in their transactional approach, presenting as all business and determined not to fall into any of the pitfalls they suspect could be out there. Hard-nosed and suffering no fools, they navigate the university with commendable precision. Much later, they might realize they still want and need all the things they had hoped for from the beginning—friends, leadership opportunities, a sense of being somebody on their campus. These things don't just happen, and they certainly don't happen as a result of playing it safe.

To a great extent, succeeding in college requires learning how to make the most of your environment. Successful students use the support systems that surround them and leverage their resources. Encourage your student to take the constructive risks listed below toward building a meaningful community on their new campus.

Participate in Community-Building Events

Regardless of how many years of college your student has under their belt, they are still new to this place, and they need friends as much as anyone. Transfer students often assume that the people around them are all well-established and already have all the friends they need, but this is probably not true. Encourage your student to lean in, explore, and find community. Orientation programs, peer mentorship programs, clubs, fraternity/sorority life, and campus employment all offer easy avenues to meet people.

Advocate for Yourself

While all students benefit enormously from learning to advocate for themselves, transfer students in particular will benefit from taking personal responsibility for their degree progress. Transferring course credits can be tricky. Course credit might initially be assessed as "elective" credit, but if your student believes it should count toward a core or major requirement, they need to speak up, starting with an academic advisor. Most universities will offer an academic adjustment process. If your student does not carefully review how their credits transferred over, they run the risk of repeating coursework, adding time and money to their degree process.

It is also important to be persistent. If your student believes that a class they took should have fulfilled more than elective credit and their academic advisor is not helpful, they can seek out the department chair for their major and inquire again. Their ability to represent their academic experience and build a case for themselves may be well worth the time, even if it requires corresponding with faculty from their previous campus to acquire the original syllabus or for help translating the value of the course they completed to their new institution.

Know Your Resources

Academic advisors are important for all students, but they are critical for transfer students. In most cases, the academic advisor will be the single resource who can connect your student to all key academic resources needed to navigate degree requirements.

Other vital resources should be identified based on what your student has experienced so far. What were the most significant hurdles for them at their last university? If they struggled with time management and study skills, for example, they need to identify support to build these skill sets. When in doubt, they can ask an academic advisor where to find resources for academic skill-building. If they previously struggled with a specific subject, such as chemistry or writing, they can seek out subject-specific support. In this case, their professors are often the best place to start. The student who is brave enough to step up and introduce themselves to the professor teaching the class that daunts them most will benefit enormously. They can let their instructor know that they expect the course to be hard for them and ask what support resources they can use to stay on top of the material. This lets the professor know that they are serious about the class, and the professor can refer them to sources of support.

Encourage your student to build relationships with academic advisors, professors, and other academic support systems early, as it is most effective at the beginning of the term before issues might arise. Your student may insist that they want to "see how it goes," hopeful that they won't struggle this time. Push back. Reaching out to the professor only after things have gone off the rails will not produce the same results. Worst case? They reach out early and then discover they didn't need help!

Leverage Your Newness

The transfer student predictably assumes that they are not like the others when, in reality, most schools are home to a significant number of transfer students. Your student may tell you that everyone already has friends or everyone knows how things work already, which is certainly not the case. Transfer students can even take advantage of their newness and introduce themselves to peers in class. They may be surprised when someone responds with, "This is my first semester here, too!"

Remind them also that just because many of their classmates have been at the school since their first term, it doesn't mean they are finished finding friends. Friend groups flex each year, and just about everyone is hungry for a little more kindness and a lot more social connection. Plus, experienced students might love to show a transfer student around campus or introduce them to a beloved club.

Take Advantage of Opportunities

Recent high school graduates who enter college together can take some comfort in feeling in step with their peers. Orientation programs can accurately assume a lot about these students and design programs that meet many of their social and academic needs. Transfer students are more diverse and harder to pigeonhole and therefore a bit harder to design for. Encourage your student to take advantage of everything the university offers to help them acclimate, but help them understand in advance that they may need to actively try to meet people and build community. They are less likely to stumble upon their new best friend in the form of a roommate or a conversation partner in an orientation group than someone right out of high school.

Don't let your student forget that they have something going for them that the average new student does not: They have experience and maturity born out of playing the big game of life. They know how important it is to understand their resources, to take advantage of opportunities, and to build a support system.

Closing Advice

For your student to be successful, they need to reflect on why they decided to transfer in the first place and put energy into understanding their new environment. By having conversations with them prior to their move to a new campus, you can help motivate your transfer student to seek out the things that will make their transition smoother. Have them mark their calendar for transfer student events, involvement fairs, and any other opportunities to receive support. Encourage them to find an on-campus job and connect with their advisor and professors. Remind them that, while they are an experienced student, this specific experience is still new.

Conversation Starters

- What went well academically/socially at your first school? What was challenging?

- What are the biggest lessons you learned about being a college student?

- What do you want to do differently this time around?

- How do you plan to make friends and find a community at your new school?

- What do you expect to be your biggest challenge in transferring? How are you going to find support in that area?

Conclusion

Colleges and universities see the value that transfer students bring to their campuses, including their experiences, resilience, and passion for education. A transfer is not without its challenges, however. Moving, learning new systems, making new friends, and starting over can be exhausting and hard. But while they might at times struggle during this transition, your transfer student is not alone and certainly not overlooked.

Whatever the reason for the transfer, your student has the skills needed to make it stick this time around. Your support, along with meaningful questions and guidance, can help them make the decision that is best for them and ensure they are successful. Help them reflect, put themselves out there, and move forward. They've got this, and you do, too!

www.ingramcontent.com/pod-product-compliance
Lightning Source LLC
Chambersburg PA
CBHW011746020426
42331CB00014B/3294